EARLY RAILWAYS

DISCOVERIES AND INVENTIONS

Rodney Dale

OXFORD UNIVERSITY PRESS

Photographic Acknowledgements

All illustrations in this book have been taken from out-of-copyright material in the British Library's collections, with the exception of those which carry a credit line in the accompanying caption. Patents are numbered and dated for ease of reference.

OXFORD UNIVERSITY PRESS

Oxford New York Toronto
Delhi Bombay Calcutta Madras Karachi
Kuala Lumpur Singapore Hong Kong Tokyo
Nairobi Dar es Salaam Cape Town
Melbourne Auckland Madrid
and associated companies in
Berlin Ibadan

First published in 1994 by The British Library. First published in North and South America by Oxford University Press, Inc., 200 Madison Avenue, New York, New York 10016 by arrangement with The British Library.
Oxford is a registered trademark of Oxford University Press

Library of Congress Cataloging-in-Publication Data

Dale, Rodney, 1933-
  Early Railways /Rodney Dale.
  64p. 24.6 x 18.9 cm. — (Discoveries and Inventions)
  Includes bibliographical references and index.
  Summary: Surveys the early history of railroads, describing advances in surveying and track construction, the intricacies of timetabling, the first tickets and ticketing systems, etc.
  ISBN 0-19-521003-4. — ISBN 0-19-521007-7 (pbk.)
  1. Railroads — Juvenile literature. [1. Railroads.] I. Title.
II. Series.
TF148.D35 1993
385 — dc20   93-18984
                                        CIP
                                        AC

Designed by Roger Davies
Set in Palatino on Ventura
Printed in Italy

Contents

The need for a transport system

There be three things that make a nation prosperous, a fertile soil, busy workshops and easy conveyance for men and commodities from one place to another.

So wrote the philospher Francis Bacon some five centuries ago. On one side of the Atlantic Ocean, Britain had fertile soil and, as the 19th century dawned, busy workshops, and steam engines to power those workshops. On the other side was the vast American continent waiting to be exploited. The two countries had very different characteristics and very different needs from their transport systems. In 1800, Britain had about twice the population of America in about one tenth of the area.

1800 data

	Area (sq miles)	Population
United States	891,364	5,308,483
Britain	88,168	10,500,956

What was lacking was a reliable and convenient means of moving things around, the more so when – as in America – distances were so vast and the land so unpopulated. In England the far-sighted Duke of Bridgewater (1736–1803) had invested a fortune in building a canal to carry his coals from his mines to Manchester – a venture which eventually paid handsomely.

Britain was well supplied with rivers along which, by a happy fact, larger towns tended to grow. There was thus the makings of a waterway system and, in the second half of the 18th century and into the 19th, a canal mania hit the country, whereby rivers were joined by artificial watercourses, and smaller reaches made navigable, until a respectable network provided a communications system to give a much-needed impetus to industrialization.

However, the notion of 'customer care' seems to have been sadly lacking. It could, and often did, take longer to carry goods from the port of Liverpool to the city of Manchester, than it took to bring the same goods (by sailing ship) from New York to Liverpool.

Detention in warehouses, from want of barges, or stress of business, or stress of weather or caprice of manager, or bargee, or want of water, closing of route, and various other reasons, had caused a tremendous accumulation of material, but the canal people cared not if mills stood still and hands stood idle and hungry. It was not the canal manager who cared; his company would only carry timber – and then only one kind. Go where else you please; please don't bring your bales here!

Carriage by road was little better. The lack of a proper nationwide view had prevented the construction of an adequate road system connecting hamlets, villages, towns and cities. True, there were 'turnpike trusts' charged with collecting tolls to improve stretches of road but, because of the parochial outlook, there was little incentive to build a system which appeared to benefit few people. As the need to transport goods from manufacturing centres to users grew, it was met by canals.

In the case of the failure of the Liverpool–Manchester canal cited above, it might be thought that the road carriers would have stepped in and taken advantage of the need. But not a bit of it; according to the same

The pack-horse convoy equipped with bells to help keep it together and warn oncoming convoys of its approach.

A basket coach (1780), so called because of the rear basket in which a few passengers could travel in relative discomfort.

A travelling craftsman with well-equipped pack saddle. He would be carrying materials to meet orders taken on his previous round.

The gateway to the future: a magic portal between the horse-drawn vehicle and the steam train, symbolized by the imposing entrance to Euston Square Station on the London & Birmingham Railway in 1837.

commentator, those who tried another of the transport companies 'who lived and fattened on the tolls of road carriage' were met in the same spirit of obstruction: We will carry it or not, as we please, at our own time, take our time too; if you don't like our terms and charges try elsewhere. Canals were built in America too, but there water transport suffered from a variety of other short-comings: the difficulty of travelling against the current (before steam boats were introduced), freezing in the winter, and drought in the summer.

But salvation was at hand: a go-ahead system, to be based on the growing technology of steam power, pro-moted by private companies with a need to stay in business and make a profit, building and owning their own roads – in short, the railway system.

For some time, collieries, quarries and ironworks had been running loads on rails, and a far-sighted per-son – presumably not a canal or road-haulage operator – could have seen the railways coming.

One such far-sighted person was a commercial trav-eller, Thomas Gray of Nottingham, England. He saw the 'trains' of coal wagons at a colliery and exclaimed:

Why are not these roads laid down all over England, and steam engines employed to convey goods and passengers along them, to supersede horsepower?' His prejudiced friend replied: 'Propose that to the nation, and see what you'll get by it. Why, sir, you will be worried to death for your pains.

But Gray was not discouraged; he saw all around him expanding commerce, struggling to extend its channels, the Bridgewater Canal blocked, the burden of monopoly greater than the trade could bear. Machinery was being driven by steam, and production increased in consequence. Inventors busy in the textile trade had given an impetus to cotton manufacture. Here, too, was needed an alternative means of transport to the expensive and slow waterways.

The canal capitalists bore the seeds of their own downfall. They made a favour of transporting goods, and handled them in the most cavalier manner. Managers actually kept people waiting while they decided whether they would, or would not, take certain freights. They abused their authority and thus – for some unaccountable reason – undermined their own business and their future.

Nevertheless, when Thomas Gray published his 'Observations' his pleas were called crochets; his views regarded as 'visionary'. Gray pressed his subject home on all occasions and, according to one account, 'enveloped you in steam' on the slightest provocation. Thus must Gray be regarded as a railroad pioneer; he certainly seems to have been one of the warmest and most original advocates and designers of the railroad.

When an old friend of his returned to England from Brussels in 1818, he found that no one was allowed to see Gray, for he 'had some mysterious work in hand which could not be named'. Gray's work occupied him for years and he believed that it would revolutionize society. Mrs Gray, however, did not seem to share her husband's enthusiasms, saying that 'the writings' would 'make him ill again', and she continued: 'I ask you what good will it do him that, as he maintains, he is busying himself with the happiness of humankind.' At last, Gray published his 'Observations of the general iron railway, or land steam conveyance, to supersede the necessity for horses in all public vehicles.'

'Here' exclaims Gray 'is the mainspring of the civilisation of the world; all distances shall disappear, people shall come here from all parts of the continent without danger and without fatigue; distances will be reduced one half; companies will be formed; the system shall extend over all countries. The discovery will be on a par with that of printing!' He was, of course, condemned as a madman, and it was left to others to put his schemes into practice.

A 'primitive train': the 'coach' is clearly just that.

What is a railway?

A 'way' originally meant a traveller's path. A 'road' way is one along which you ride – or walk, or pull a wheeled vehicle; it needs a reasonable surface if the passage is to be smooth.

Wheeled vehicles tend to cut deeper and deeper ruts as they pass, especially if the ground is wet. The secret of a good road is good drainage, which the Romans well understood when they built their military roads in Europe and Britain. Their roads have survived in some places because of the meticulous way in which they were designed and built.

It is clear that a level surface on which horses can walk, and cart wheels can run, reduces the amount of effort needed, and as heavier and heavier loads had to be moved, so the need for an easier passage increased. It was the development of mining – and particularly coal mining – which spurred the laying of 'rail-roads' or 'rail-ways' – roads or ways on which rails were laid so that the vehicles thereon would run smoothly.

The words 'railroad' and 'railway' emerged in Britain at about the same time (1775) and were used interchangeably. With the opening of the first passenger lines (1825–1830) the words soon gained their present meaning covering the whole outfit – not just the track, but the locomotives, rolling stock, buildings and all. In America, the word 'railroad' took over; in Britain it was 'railway'.

Early tracks

In Britain the road specially prepared for fast or heavy traffic (by no means the same thing) goes back nearly 500 years. It was reported in 1555 that there was a 'tram from the west end of the Bridge Gate in Barnard Castle' (Country Durham) for whose repair Ambrose Middleton left 20 shillings in his will. The word 'tram' seems to have been used in the north of England and the south of Scotland as descriptive of both the special track and the trucks that ran on it.

The track was of timbers laid lengthways and the trucks were hauled by men or horses. Tracks of this sort were found in Northumberland by Roger North in 1676; on them, 'carts with four rowlets' carried the coals from the collieries to the Tyne. North wrote:

Men have pieces of ground between the colliery and the river. They sell leave to lead coals over the ground. The manner of the carriage is by laying rails of timber from the colliery down

A section of early American railroad: iron straps nailed to wooden stringers fastened to wooden sleepers. The rolling action of the wheels imparted stress to the iron straps, which would sometimes break away and impale the train – and perhaps a passenger – as it passed over.

A busy curve on the 'Outram-way' at Little Eaton, Derbyshire.

'Pointers': points or switches, on the 'Outram-way' at Ticknall, Derbyshire.

to the river, exactly straight and parallel, whereby the carriage is so easy that one horse will draw four or five chaldrons of coal.

Coal production started to increase towards the end of the 17th century, as the demand for a fuel to replace wood grew, and all the early railways were associated with a need to move coal. Primitive tracks were laid alongside the River Tyne, for example, to the platform or 'staith' from which the coals were shot into the barge or 'collier'. The wooden roads were quickly worn out by the continual friction of the 'wayne' or wagon wheels, and the surface needed constant upkeep.

As the traffic grew, cast-iron plates were laid over the surface of the wood block tracks to make them more durable. At first, simple flat plates were used; later they were provided with flanges to keep the wheels of the trucks from running off. The dates of these developments are uncertain, but in 1734 cast-iron wheels with an inner flange were in use near Bath, and about the same time cast-iron plates were laid on the tracks.

Iron wheels were introduced in 1753, but took some time to become accepted. As the improvement in rail and wheels continued, tyres were made slightly grooved so as to fit the rail more closely. However, this design was abandoned when it was found that wear made the fit too tight and the friction too great.

The next idea was to use plates of iron with a flange or 'trammel' to stop the wheels from running off. In 1767 the old railway at Coalbrookdale had inner flanges. In 1776, John Carr laid a cast-iron plateway at the Duke of Norfolk's Nunnery Colliery near Sheffield, Yorkshire, with the flanges outside.

'The making and use of iron rail roads were the first of my inventions and were introduced at the Sheffield Colliery about 21 years ago' wrote John Carr in his *Coal Viewer* in 1797. The invention of the flanges was also claimed by an ironfounder named Benjamin Outram. Outram cast the plates at his foundry and sent his 'plate layers' to lay them along the route. (The title 'plate layer' was used for people who laid railways long after the original plates had passed into oblivion.) Because the improved running surface needed fewer horses and men to manoeuvre the wagons, the colliers felt threatened and broke up the plates and burned the wooden tracks. Outram had to hide in a nearby wood for three days and nights 'until the fury of the populace had abated'.

In 1785, William Jessop, a pupil of the great 18th-century engineer John Smeaton (1724–92), had the idea of laying transverse 'sleepers' of wood on which were laid separate rails, fastened down with spikes. Jessop's rails were a yard (0.9m) in length and weighed about 40 lb (18kg). They were double flanged in section, with the lower flange spreading out to form a foot through which they were spiked to the sleepers.

The following year, Jessop laid down the first track using this construction between the Loughborough Canal and Nanpantan in Leicestershire. The rolling stock for use on this railway had flanged wheels – thus Jessop may be credited with establishing the principle which lasts to this day. Although William Jessop and Benjamin Outram were partners, each of them appears to have boosted his own invention at the expense of the other. As we know, Outram's pattern was soon forgotten – except that some have sought to preserve his memory by suggesting that the word 'tram' was based on his name.

Developments in America were slower, because of the longer distances and the later colonization. A four-mile (6.4km) railroad was laid in 1826 to transport granite from quarries at Quincy to Boston for building the Bunker Hill monument. The rails were of wood, fastened to stone sleepers, and the wagons were pulled by horses.

The modern era was ushered in two centuries ago when, in 1797, rails were cast without the feet in the Newcastle coal field. They were carried on 'chairs', and locked in place with wooden 'keys'. There have been a number of significant developments since then. First came rolled steel rails, far more durable than cast iron which is unsuitable for heavier and heavier trains running at higher and higher speeds. Rolled rails were produced in 60 foot (18.3m) lengths and each length was joined to the next with a flat plate bolted to both.

Because the rails expand as they get hotter, they were arranged to butt up tight in the hottest weather, and of course a gap would appear as they contracted in the winter. The continual expansion and contraction would work the keys loose, so a platelayer would have to patrol the line at intervals to knock them back again. Various methods other than chairs and keys were tried to obviate the loosening, including spring-steel spikes fastening the foot of the rail direct to the sleeper.

The interaction between train and track has been the subject of thorough and continuing studies. One obvious problem arises from the gap between the rails; pounded continually by rolling wheels, the ends become deformed, and the deformation exacerbates the problem. An answer was found in continuously welded rails (CWR) which were long thought to be impossible to achieve because they would buckle in summer – until the appropriate materials and methods of fixing were determined. It was thought also that the resilience of wood was essential to effective sleepers, but the far more durable precast concrete sleepers are now widely used. Chairs and keys have given way to elastic spikes.

The first railroads, then, were of wood, and the wagons were drawn by horses. Iron wheels on iron roads increased the adhesive force, while the resistance was very small – hence the adoption of the tram or railroad. Perhaps the extraordinary thing is that it took so long to adapt this mode of transport to carrying passengers as well as freight.

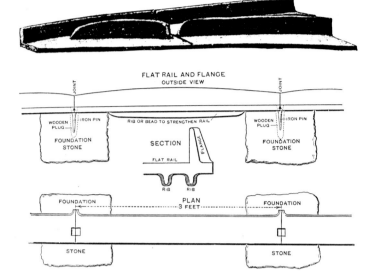

Outram's Ticknall tram rail (1799): casting of points section, which enables a wagon to pass from one track to another.

A 'plateway': a flat rail with vertical flange to retain the running wheels. The rails are pinned into wooden plugs in blocks of stone – which may be more durable than wooden sleepers.

Wylam Colliery rail of 1808. The flange is still on the rail rather than on the wheel, and the rail is keyed into a groove in a stone block with a wooden wedge.

Birkinshaw rail and chair with wedging key (1820). This method of locating and fixing rails was widely used for well over a century.

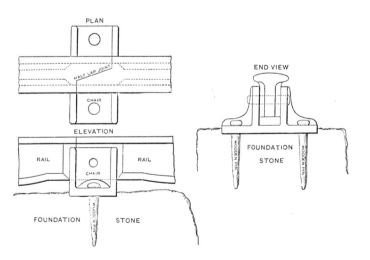

In an attempt to prevent wear on the joints between rails, Stephenson and Losh patented a half-lap joint in 1816. A pin secures the two rail ends in the chair, and the chair is screwed into wooden inserts in the foundation stone.

Some early lines

In 1799 it was proposed to lay a railway line from London to Portsmouth – an ambitious undertaking, for the distance is over 70 miles (112 km). The first stage of this line was proposed by the Surrey Iron Railway Company which obtained its Act of Parliament in 1801. This was the first railway company, the first public railway, and the first Railway Act so-called, although it was not the first Act in which a railway was authorized. The first section of the line was opened on 1 June 1804, and ran from Wandsworth to Croydon across Mitcham Common, a distance of 9.5 miles (15.3 km). The extension, for which an Act was obtained in 1803, ran from Croydon to Merstham (about the same distance).

The Surrey rails were four inches (10 cm) wide and one inch (25.4 mm) thick, with an arched flange half an inch (12.7 mm) thick and three and a half inches (89 mm) high resting direct on stone block sleepers. The gauge was four foot seven inches (1.4 m) measured outside the flange; inside it was about four foot six inches (1.37 m). The four-wheeled wagons were five feet (1.52 m) wide, two feet (0.61 m) deep and eight feet (2.44 m) long and were worked by horses. The Company made its money by charging tolls.

The gauge of the railways

No one knows why the railway gauge (the distance between the rails) in Great Britain and America is four foot eight and a half inches (1.41 m). Some say that George Stephenson (1781–1848) measured the distance between the centres of the old Roman stoneways in the neighbourhood of his home area of Newcastle upon Tyne; others say that he measured the distance between the wheels of a farm cart.

Certainly, wheeled vehicles tended to have the same track (the distance between the points of contact of the wheels with the ground) because, unpleasant as it was for wheeled vehicles to keep making the ruts deeper and deeper on the poorer roads, it was even more unpleasant to try to traverse such roads with a non-standard track, which could – and did – result in smashed wheels and overturned vehicles.

George Stephenson (1781–1848), 'the father of the railways'.

Isambard Kingdom Brunel (1806–1859), engineer of the Great Western Railway.

Great Western engine of 1838 with large driving wheel, domed firebox and prominent safety valve and whistle, just behind the funnel.

Some say that the early plate ways were laid to a 'round' gauge of five feet, and that placing the flanges on the wheels instead of on the track reduced the gauge to four feet eight and a half inches (1.44 m).

There are many different gauges over the world: Ireland at five foot three inches (1.60m), India at five foot six inches (1.68m), and America now the same as in Great Britain – four foot eight and a half inches (1.41m). This is probably due to the fact that Peter Heming, the chief engineer of the Mohawk & Hudson Railroad (chartered 1826, opened 1831), was sent to England to study railroad practice, and that some of the early locomotives were imported from England.

Notwithstanding this, the early piecemeal development of American railroads resulted in a variety of gauges – up to the six feet (1.83m) of the Erie Railroad.

As the network began to spread, and lines began to meet, the need to transfer passengers and freight from one train to another at places where the gauge changed became increasingly frustrating. Standard-gauge railroads were at an advantage, and made arrangements for through traffic on their lines. Non-standard operators lost business, and eventually the standard gauge was adopted throughout. America was able to build much larger locomotives and more capacious coaches than those in Britain, in the early days at least, because space was at less of a premium, and more room could be left on each side of and above the tracks.

In England the engineer of the Great Western Railway (GWR), Isambard Kingdom Brunel (1806–59), who always tried to do things on a grand scale, decided that he would use a 'broad' gauge of seven feet

The up 'Dutchman' passing Worle junction, Somerset, at 60 mph. The picture shows the problems of building – and drawing – mixed-gauge switches, or points.

(2.13m). He believed that a seven-foot gauge was best 'from a scientific point of view' and more important than uniformity with other lines: the ride would be more comfortable, the carriages more roomy, and the centre of gravity of the engines lower – all of which would make his railway safer.

Moreover, there was some hint that, because the GWR (long dubbed 'God's Wonderful Railway') was breaking new ground in the West Country, it would be able to maintain its monopoly by its unique gauge. But it was not to be. Broad and standard gauge met in 1844, and the disadvantage was at once apparent. A Royal Commission report the same year stated that, notwithstanding many recognized advantages in the broad gauge, uniformity was so important that, the narrow

gauge mileage being seven-eighths of the whole, it should be preferred to the broad. Nevertheless, the GWR continued to build broad track to Penzance, Milford Haven, Hereford, Worcester and even Wolverhampton.

In 1869, the GWR had to concede, and started by laying a third rail between the other two so that both broad- and standard-gauge locomotives and rolling stock could use the same track. But it was too out of step with the rest of the system to continue to be viable. Transferring passengers or goods and livestock from a standard to a broad gauge wagon (or vice versa), was just not economical. The GWR had to take up its third rail and convert completely to the standard gauge in October 1892.

For obvious reasons the rail nearest the platform was left in place and the outer one moved inwards. This left more room between the tracks for signals, which were on the outside on other railways. Today, the unwitting foresight of Brunel in choosing the broad gauge, so providing a wider-than-normal track bed, enables high-speed trains to run on tracks with less curvature than might otherwise be needed.

Narrowing the broad gauge at Plymouth Station, 1892. By that time, there were 423 miles of main and branch line remaining between Paddington, London and Penzance, Cornwall. Much of the line was single track, which demanded a carefully-planned conversion, with thousands of 'navvies' (pick-and-shovel men; short for navigators) ready to spring into action as soon as the last broad-gauge stock had been cleared.

The steam engine

A 'locomotive' is a machine which moves under its own power (or, as we now say, under its own steam). Steam was the power of the Industrial Revolution, as coal was the fuel – both literally and metaphorically. The first steam engines were built by the Cornishman Thomas Newcomen (1663–1729) and his associates at the beginning of the 18th century to pump water from flooded mines. These machines were ponderous and inefficient. Power was provided by condensing steam to water under a moveable piston in a cylinder, whereupon atmospheric pressure would push the piston down. This would pull down on a pivoted beam, whose other end would raise the pump rod, and with it a charge of water. The piston was then returned to the top of its stroke by the weight of the descending pump rod, rather than by the pressure of steam admitted to the cylinder for the next stroke.

Half a century after the first Newcomen engines were installed, the 28-year-old James Watt (1736–1819) was asked to repair a demonstration model at Glasgow University. He found that the engine was so inefficient that it would operate only for a few strokes before running out of steam. Watt realized that condensing the steam in the cylinder was wasteful of energy, for 80 per cent of the energy in the new charge of steam was used to heat up the cold metal. (True, full scale Newcomen engines were no more efficient, but the ratio of surface area to volume of the cylinder was smaller.)

Watt's first improvement was the separate condenser; the cylinder was insulated and kept at working temperature with a steam jacket. He also used expanding steam, rather than air pressure, to move the piston.

After various vicissitudes, Watt went into partnership with a Birmingham businessman, Matthew Boulton (1728–1809), and continued his experiments at

A Newcomen steam engine. The onion-shaped boiler a is beneath the cylinder c. The piston in the cylinder is pushed down by air pressure when the steam beneath it is condensed by admitting cold water. This raises the pump-rod m.

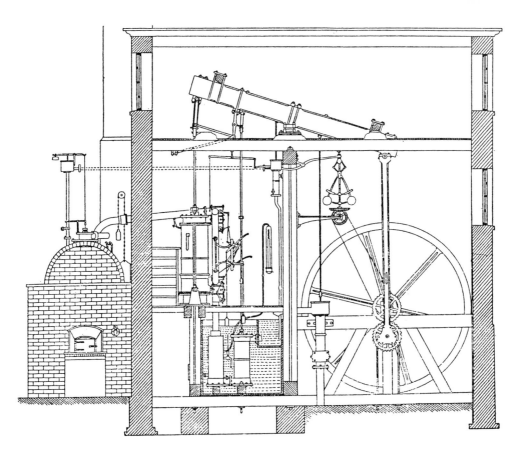

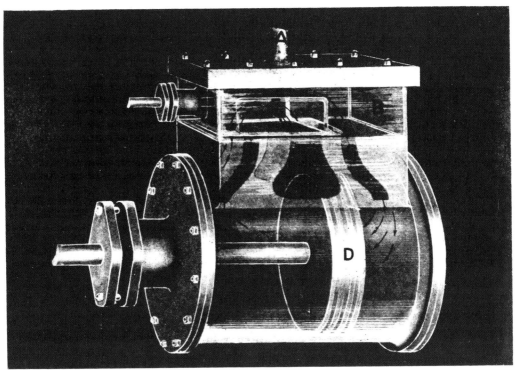

Watt's double-acting rotative steam engine of 1784. It is double acting in that steam acts on each side of the piston alternately. It is rotative in that it drives a rotating flywheel via the sun-and-planet gear. The balls of the governor, which regulates the speed, are seen above the flywheel.

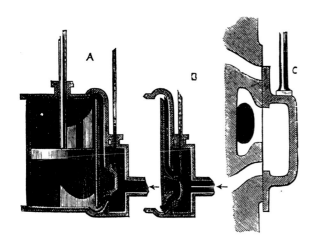

Another diagram of the slide valve. Note that the slide may move either in the same direction as, or in the opposite direction to, the piston. This property is used for reversing the engine.

The cylinder – the 'soul of the steam engine'. Steam enters the steam chest B through the pipe A. The mouth of port C is uncovered, so steam passes into the cylinder, pushing the piston D to the left. This exhausts the old steam from the previous stroke through the port E into the inside of the slide valve F, and thence to the exhaust port G. As the piston moves to the left, the slide valve moves to the right until port C becomes connected to the exhaust port, and port G opens for the fresh steam, which then pushes the piston from left to right.

Boulton's Soho Works in 1775. It was about this time that Watt began to develop the double-acting rotative engine – double acting in that steam pushed first one side of the piston, then the other; rotative in that double action enabled the piston to push the beam up as well as pull it down, necessitating a positive drive from the piston, and making a crank and flywheel output possible. As it happened, James Pickard had patented the arguably unpatentable crank, so that Watt had to find an alternative – this was the sun-and-planet drive, which turns the flywheel at twice the speed of the crank.

The locomotive

The step from the ponderous beam engine to something compact and wieldy enough to be a locomotive engine is reasonably simple (at least with hindsight). There is no reason why the piston should not act

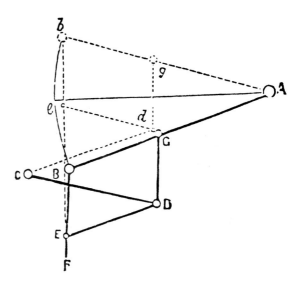

In a single-acting engine (see page 15), the piston pulls on a chain carried on an arc on the end of the beam so as to maintain a vertical position above the piston. Since the chain cannot be pushed, Watt invented his parallel motion so that the piston rod always keeps a vertical position. AB is the beam, and the links ensure that point E stays on a vertical line.

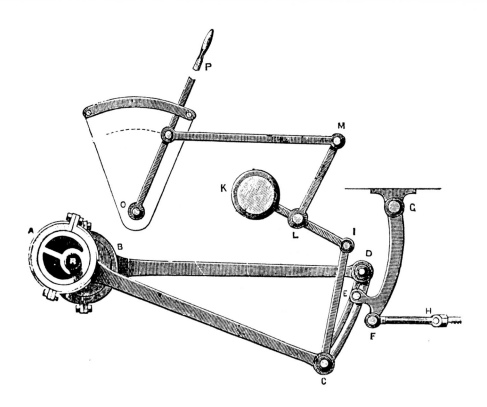

Robert Stephenson's link motion served two purposes: to reverse the engine, and to use the expansive power of steam more economically. The driving shaft R carries two eccentrics A and B (bottom left). As the eccentrics rotate, the ends of the slide bar CD move backwards and forwards relative to one another. A lever pivoted to the chassis of the locomotive at G works in the slot of the slide bar at E and controls the motion of the slide valve in the steam chest via the link FH. The driver of the engine controls the position of CD in relation to point E by means of the handle P and the linkages. In the position shown, the motion of the slide valve is affected mainly by eccentric B, and hardly at all by eccentric A. If the lever P is placed in its mid position – so that E is on the mid-point between C and D – the slide valve will not move at all. If the lever P is pulled right over to the left, the motion of the slide valve will be controlled by eccentric A rather than by eccentric B. We have here a mechanism for deciding which side of the piston steam will be admitted – and thus capable of reversing the engine – and for shortening the travel of the slide valve as the engine gains speed, thus conserving steam.

directly on the crank, either via a crosshead, or from the piston rod of an oscillating cylinder. There is no reason why the crank should not be connected directly to the running wheels. However, a great deal of engineering is needed to put such ideas into practice.

Cugnot

In 1763, the Frenchman Nicholas Cugnot built an experimental steam-powered carriage. Its original purpose was for pulling artillery into position in battle, but the design was such that it ran out of steam after a few minutes and everything had to wait while pressure got up again. Another design fault lay in mounting the boiler and works over the single steering front wheel which, as anyone who has tried to ride a bicycle with a heavily-laden basket will know, is a recipe for disaster. It is no surprise that, when the engine ran out of control and fell over, it was shut away.

Cornish engineers

The scene shifts to the birthplace of the steam locomotive, Cornwall. In Redruth lived two inventive men

Nicolas Cugnot's steam carriage, with its enormous boiler generating steam to drive a Newcomen-type engine connected to the front (steering) wheel. The mass on the front axle made it difficult to control, and the engine was so inefficient that the vehicle had to keep stopping to raise a new head of steam.

who gave the development of the steam locomotive its next impetus – William Murdock (1754–1839) and Richard Trevithick (1771–1833).

William Murdock

Murdock was employed by Boulton & Watt, and lived in Cornwall to look after his employers' interests there. (Boulton & Watt made their money by collecting royalties from users of their engines, rather than by building and installing those engines.) Richard Trevithick had learnt some of the enginewright's craft from Murdock (17 years his senior), but thereafter made a living by improving upon – or evading – Watt's patents.

After 18 years in Cornwall, Murdock left in 1799 to become superintendent of Boulton & Watt's Soho Works in Birmingham. By that time, Trevithick was employed making fuel-saving improvements to an engine at Wheal Jane Mine, and was soon appointed engineer at Ding Dong Mine near Penzance. It is possible that Murdock was 'recalled' to Birmingham because Watt was concerned that he might be spending too much time on developing a locomotive, work of which Watt disapproved. Before sailing for Quebec in 1759, one John Robison had been working with Watt on the idea of a locomotive, and Watt included the use of steam for land transport in his patent. However, he abandoned the idea and discouraged experiments among his staff at the Soho works in Birmingham. Murdock, however, working in Cornwall, had a freer hand to pursue his own interests.

Murdock built a small model and – so the story goes – took it one evening to the narrow, well-kept walk leading to Redruth church. It was dark and he was alone. He lit the lamp under the boiler and got up steam. Suddenly, the locomotive started to move off, with Murdock chasing after it. Hearing shouts of terror, he found that the parson, returning from business in town, had been met on the lonely road by the 'fiery little traveller'. However, according to the parson's daughter, her father and mother, returning from town, were startled by a fizzing sound, and saw 'a little thing zig-zagging about on the road.' Fortunately Murdock, whom her parents knew well, was close behind. She understood that he wished the experiment to be kept secret, and she did not recollect ever hearing of it afterwards.

Whichever story be accepted – and the daughter's account seems more mature – it is clear that Murdock made a model, and that it moved by itself on the walk leading to Redruth church. No doubt he wished to keep his experiment secret lest Watt should find out about it; nevertheless, details of his engines were reported to his employers.

Murdock continued with his clandestine work on the self-moving engine, but it came to an end when, by a happy – or unhappy – accident Boulton, visiting Cornwall, met a coach near Exeter in which he caught sight of Murdock. The two men alighted; according to Boulton:

He said he was going to London to get men, but I soon found he was going there with his steam carriage to show it and take out a patent ... However, I prevailed upon him to return to Cornwall by the next day's diligence, and he accordingly arrived at noon, since which he hath unpacked his carriage and made it travel a mile or two in Rivers's great room, making it carry the fire shovel, poker and tongs. I think it

Murdock's model steam carriage. The smaller front wheel steers; the rear wheels have a crank in the centre of their axle, driven by a linkage from the vertical steam cylinder.

Model of William Hedley's carriage for testing adhesion (1812). The handles are geared to the axles, which carry smooth wheels. The vehicle may carry a load, or be hooked on to another vehicle. If the road is level, the adhesion is found to be perfectly adequate for a locomotive pulling a heavy train.

fortunate that I met him, as I am persuaded I can cure him of the disorder or turn the evil to good. At least I shall prevent a mischief that would have been the consequence of his journey to London.

Boulton and Watt had enough to do in their own business, and they wished neither to lose Murdock nor to embark on another venture that might be risky. William Murdock was thus deprived by the policy of his firm of the honour of introducing the locomotive. Perhaps one of his errors was to back high-pressure steam, which Watt had always been against. Watt's engines worked at pressures below 10 pounds per square inch (69kPa), in spite of the fact that the higher the pressure, the more energy the steam contains, and the smaller the size of the engine – and comparative smallness is, of course, a necessity in a locomotive. Perhaps, in his sixties, with so much invention and tradition of his own making a part of him, the old dog Watt was hardly capable of learning new tricks.

Richard Trevithick

Richard Trevithick, on the other hand, was a high-pressure man in more senses than one, and from his youth had been keenly interested in steam. Naturally inventive, he produced a locomotive of his own. At the age of 26, in 1797, he married and made his home at Moreton House, Redruth, where he built and tested his first model locomotive. It had a one-piece boiler and engine; hot water was poured into the boiler and a red-hot cast-iron block put into the oval flue, a practice borrowed from the old-fashioned tea urn. The engine had a vertical double-acting (steam admitted each end in turn) cylinder 1.55 inches (3.9 cm) in diameter and a stroke of 3.6 inches (9.14 cm). The cylinder was mounted inside the boiler and the piston rod ended in a guided crosshead with connecting rods to crank pins in the two four-inch driving wheels. A spur wheel on the crankshaft drove a fly wheel. For three years, Trevithick experimented with and improved upon his model before he built a full-sized machine.

Like many others of the time, Trevithick was concerned as to whether or not the wheels of a self-propelled carriage on rails should be smooth or toothed. He came to the conclusion that smooth wheels would give sufficient hold on any reasonable gradient, but he put the matter to the test by hiring the carriage that had been kept for Watt's use when he was in Redruth 16 years before. With his friend Davies Giddy (1767–1839, later to become Davies Gilbert, President of the Royal Society), Trevithick took the vehicle out on to a road near Camborne where, unharnessing the horse, they tried to work it uphill by applying their strength to the spokes of the wheel. They tried the experiment on various surfaces and found no slip, confirming Trevithick's expectations that smooth wheels would work on smooth rails. To guard his rights, he wrote in his patent of 1802: 'We do occasionally, or in certain cases, make the external periphery of the wheels uneven, by projecting heads of nails or bolts, or cross-grooves, or fittings to railroads when required; and in cases of hard pull we cause a lever, bolt or claw, to project through the rim of one or both of the said wheels, so as to take hold of the ground; but in general the ordinary structure or figure of the external surface of these wheels will be found to answer the intended purpose.'

Trevithick's full size engine was ready on Christmas Eve 1801 and the first load of passengers was moved by steam on what was known in the neighbourhood as 'Captain Dick's Puffer'. It was raining heavily, the road was rough and the gradient steep but 'she went off like a little bird', travelling three quarters of a mile (1.2 km) up Beacon Hill (to what became Camborne Railway Station) and home again. Over Christmas dinner, Trevithick and his cousin Andrew Vivian became partners and soon travelled to London with letters of introduction from Giddy to Humphry Davy (1778–1829), who in turn introduced them to Count Rumford; both helped to patent Trevithick's invention.

On 22 August 1802 Trevithick was at Coalbrookdale erecting a pumping engine whence he wrote to Giddy:

Trevithick's Pen-y-Darran locomotive. Apart from the gears, the most prominent feature of this engine is the linkage between the front end of the piston and the driving cranks. The intermediate gear drives the wheels.

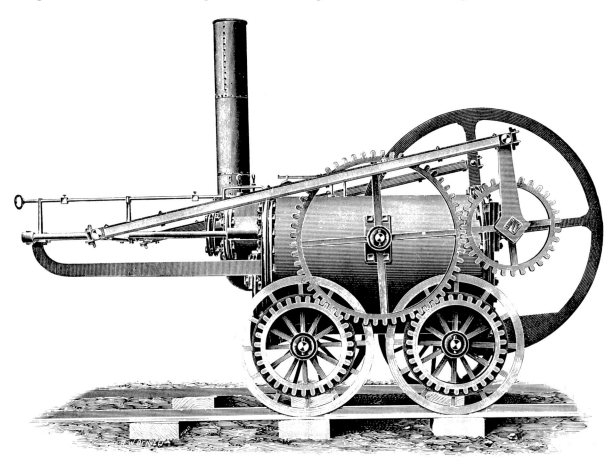

'The Dale company have begun a carriage at their own cost for the railroads, and are forcing it with all expedition.' But we know nothing more of this. Later that year, Trevithick was back in Cornwall building another locomotive which he took to London in 1803 where he learned the hard way, from running it on varieties of paving, that locomotives would run best on a smooth 'iron road'.

October 1803 found Trevithick at the Pen-y-Darran ironworks, near Merthyr Tydfil, in Wales, building the engine with which some say the railway era began. The Pen-y-Darran engine was designed for many uses and worked on the tram road for the first time on Monday 13 February 1804. Trevithick wrote to Giddy:

It worked very well and ran uphill and downhill with great ease, and was very manageable. We had plenty of steam and power . . . The engine, with water included, is about five tons. It runs up the tram road of two inches in a yard 40 strokes per minute with the empty wagons. The engine moves forward nine feet at every stroke.

This sounds quite workmanlike, but turns out to be about 4 mph (6.4 kph).

I intend to make a smaller engine for the road, as this has much more power than is wanted here. This engine is to work a hammer. We shall continue our journey on the road today with the engine until we meet Mr Homfray and the London engineer, and intend to take the horses out of the coach and draw them home. The coach axles are the same length as the engine axles so the coach will run very easily on the tram road.

The 'London engineer' had been sent by an unusually far-sighted government to see Trevithick and his locomotive with a view to ordering similar engines if this one passed certain tests. 'The wagon engine is to lift the water in the pipes, then go by itself from the pump and work a hammer, then wind coal, and lastly to go the journey on the road with a load of iron.'

The Great Run took place the following day from the Works to the Navigation House. The engine hauled ten tons of iron, five wagons, and 70 men riding on them for the whole of the journey, nine miles (14.4 km) in four hours and five minutes, without replenishing the boiler and using two cwt (102 kg) of coal. After a small repair, the engine continued working, and 10 days later was tried with 25 tons of iron.

Trevithick spent the rest of 1804 superintending the erection of his high-pressure stationary engines in various parts of the country. In September, he was at Newcastle upon Tyne arranging to supply Christopher Blackett, the owner of *The Globe* newspaper, with a locomotive for Wylam Colliery. This was erected at John Whinfield's works at Gateshead and was completed in May 1805. Like the Pen-y-Darran engine, the Gateshead engine used a steam-blast in the flue, rather than bellows, to create a draught through the firebox.

The Gateshead engine was the first with flanged wheels, but these did not suit the Wylam track which had wooden rails. In 1808, they were replaced with cast-iron rails (on which, in 1813, *Puffing Billy* ran). Trevithick's engine was taken off and used as a stationary engine, having worked satisfactorily on a temporary iron railway in Whinfield's Yard – the first engine to work on a iron edge rail. Everyone in the district interested in engineering – including George Stephenson – went to see it, and thus began the history of the locomotive in the north east of England.

Trevithick was a prolific engineer and produced several other inventions over the next ten years. He built a steam dredger for the River Thames and iron tanks for water systems. He was the engineer of the first Thames tunnel (1809). In 1811 he built the first steam threshing machine, and then a steam plough. In 1812 came his Cornish pumping engine, and in 1815 his screw propeller for steam ships – and the first water-tube boiler.

In 1808, Trevithick brought his locomotive *Catch-me-who-can* and some passenger vehicles to London. He built a circular track about 70 feet (213.3 m) in diameter, fenced it off, and charged people one shilling to ride round at about 12 mph (19.2 kph). The track was laid on longitudinal sleepers and the engine weighed over eight tons – it was more like a modern locomotive than the Trevithick's Gateshead one, for Trevithick had abandoned the spur gears and large fly wheel (which, however, survived on road traction engines and steam rollers). Presumably the experiment was ahead of its time – it was not a financial success and, when a rail broke and the locomotive overturned, Trevithick abandoned it.

John Blenkinsop

In 1811, John Blenkinsop patented (no 3,431) a rail with 'a toothed rack or longitudinal piece of cast-iron or other fit material having the teeth or protuberances or

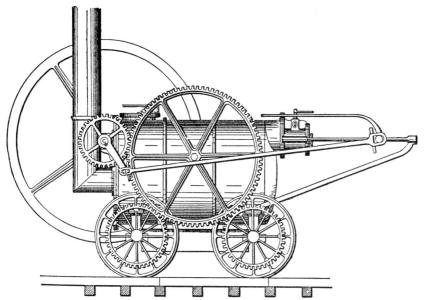

Trevithick's Wylam or 'Newcastle' locomotive – the first to have flanged wheels. This locomotive looks similar to the Pen-y-Darran model, but the gear ratios are different.

Blenkinsop's wheel with teeth or protuberances working into a racked rail mounted on chairs, British patent no 3,431 of 1811.

other parts of the nature of teeth standing either upwards, downwards or sideways' with the intervals of which 'a wheel having teeth or protuberances' would engage – as in today's mountain-climbing railways. Blenkinsop was the agent of the Middleton Colliery, and to carry the coals three and a half miles (5.6 km) to Leeds he needed toothed wheels on a road 'on which the levels were few and the gradients many'.

Blenkinsop's 'protuberances' were a series of semi-circular ears arranged along the side of the rail half an inch from the upper edge like so many small arches, each about three inches across (7.6 cm), 3/8 inch (9.6mm) thick and projecting some two and a quarter inches (5.71 cm). There were seven of these ears to each 41-inch (104.14 cm) rail. The top of the rail was smooth as were the running wheels of the engine; however, the driving wheel between the running wheels (fore and aft) worked outside the rail, not on it, its projections being rounded so as to run easily between the rounded ears. Blenkinsop patented the principle of the rack and wheel, not the engine or 'carriage' as he called it. The engines were designed and built by Matthew Murray; they had two cylinders, as recommended by Trevithick in his 1802 patent, so arranged that the cranks were at right angles to one another. This arrangement ensured that, if one piston were at top (or bottom) 'dead centre' the other would be half way along its stroke and thus ready to start the engine moving forwards or backwards as desired.

These were the first two-cylinder engines, the first with six wheels (2-2-2) and the railway was the first that was financially successful. The first engine ran

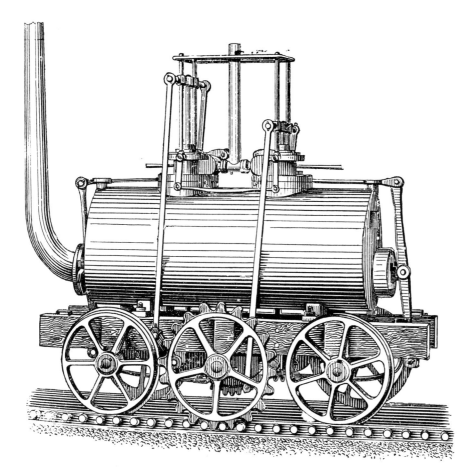

Blenkinsop's rack locomotive. The connecting rods from the cylinders (which are mounted partially inside the boiler) drive crankshafts, which transmit the power to the rack wheel by means of spur gears. The cranks are arranged so that the engine will always start.

from the colliery to the wharf at Leeds on 24 June 1812, its final load being eight wagons carrying 25 tons of coal and 50 people. In regular work, the locomotive hauled a train of as many as 30 wagons; considering the gradients and the weight of the engine (about five tons) Blenkinsop was surely correct in thinking he could not do without his 'protuberances'.

George Stephenson

In 1812, George Stephenson (1781–1848) was appointed enginewright at Killingworth High Pit at a salary of £100 a year, and in riding about inspecting the collieries he became interested in the new railway with its Blenkinsop rails and engines.

Next year, at Christopher Blackett's suggestion, William Hedley built an engine for Wylam Colliery named *Puffing Billy*. Hedley had found, by an experiment confirming Trevithick's, that smooth wheels had sufficient adhesion on smooth rails when the gradients of the track were slight. However, the first *Puffing Billy*

was a failure because its weight, supported by only four wheels, broke the cast-iron plate track. In 1815, Hedley converted *Puffing Billy* to an eight wheeler, each group of four wheels being attached to a 'bogie' or truck. In 1830 the line was re-laid with cast-iron edge rails and *Billy* reverted to four-wheels. From the first, this engine was a great improvement on the horses and was kept at work until 1862. Its sister engine *Wylam Dilly* worked until 1867. It is a tribute to the engineering of the time that pioneer locomotives should stay in service for nearly half a century.

George Stephenson could hardly avoid studying the Wylam engines working on the track that ran past the cottage in which he had been born in 1781. He concluded that he could improve upon them, and in 1814 he built his first locomotive: *Blucher*. This was not very successful – until he turned the waste steam into the funnel as Trevithick had done, thus doubling the power of the engine. Stephenson's next locomotive was the Killingworth engine of 1815. At first, this had

William Hedley's *Puffing Billy* in its four-wheeled form. The central crankshaft drives the wheels via spur gears.

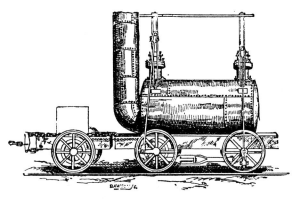

George Stephenson's engine of 1815. The cylinders are mounted partially inside the boiler; each drives one of the axles.

coupling rods working inside cranks between the two wheels, but when one of the crank axles became bent he replaced the rods with sprockets and chains; he used the same drive in his engine of 1816.

In 1817, the Duke of Portland ordered a Stephenson engine for his Kilmarnock & Troon line, the first locomotive to be worked in Scotland, but the cast-iron wheels damaged the cast-iron track and were ingeniously replaced – by wooden ones.

In the year the first engine went to Scotland a railway was projected from Stockton-on-Tees to Darlington. Thus it was that the railway age in Britain – as most people think of it – really began. Under Stephenson's enthusiasm and influence railways rapidly developed from horse to steam working.

Taking stock

Some commentators saw the modern railroad leaping, fully equipped, from the fertile minds of mine owners and their engineers. But the process was much slower than that. Certainly, the Duke of Bridgewater was concerned at the effect of the emerging railroad on his canals. He is said to have commented that the canals 'will last my time, but I do not like the look of those tram roads' and he confirmed his opinion by emphatically condemning the latter. But, as we have seen, there were tramways, railroads – call them what you will – long before the Duke's time.

Whether worked by humans or horses, it is much easier to move smooth-wheeled vehicles along smooth ways than it is to move them on common roads. The principle of the railway was fully understood before the power of steam was employed either in stationary engines to pull the 'trains' of wagons along, or in the locomotive whose early history we have already covered.

The idea of using steam power on the Surrey Iron Railway attracted considerable attention. Pumping engines were common: James Watt had made many important discoveries and had foreseen the steam locomotive – though his insistence on using 'safe' low

Measuring altitude using Admiral Fortin's very accurate barometer in travelling form. The art of surveying, especially applicable to digging tunnels starting from both ends simultaneously, was developed by the canal engineers and carried on by the railway engineers whose embankments and cuttings were on an even grander scale than those of their predecessors.

pressure, low-energy steam militated against locomotive development.

It was a Mr James who went to Mr Sanders of Liverpool and offered to survey a suggested line from Manchester to Liverpool. Mr Sanders agreed, paid the expenses, and the survey was made in 1822; the plan, however, was allowed to drop.

The Stockton & Darlington line

Meanwhile, an association of the Society of Friends (Quakers) in Durham had already projected a tramway, and had obtained – not without difficulty – an Act of Parliament in 1821. This Act was 'For the passage of wagons and other carriages from Stockton to Witton Park Colliery, Darlington.' It was originally projected as a tramroad, and it could be used by the public with cattle and carriages by arrangement. The projector of this line was Mr Edward Pease who lived to the age of 92 and saw the advantages claimed for the railway system fully realised.

When George Stephenson heard about the proposed Stockton–Darlington line he went to see Pease to discuss his vision of the developing railway system, and to advocate a rail-way rather than a tram-way. He went on to astonish Pease by suggesting that locomotive engines rather than horses should be used for pulling the trains of wagons. Stephenson departed; Pease pondered. No one would credit a locomotive; a horse was much better. Lord Eldon generously – but very foolishly – decided to 'eat all the coals the railway will carry'. Although the Act was obtained in 1821, the first public railway between Stockton-on-Tees and Darlington was not opened until 1825. It is easy with hindsight to wonder what the hold-up was; hard to imagine the opposition to railway building especially from those landowners through whose property the proposed lines would run. All resisted the railways; agitators told them that no one would need horses soon and the farmers would be ruined! There was also opposition from the canal-owners, who had the monopoly of the most satisfactory transport system of the time, and from the City Fathers controlling those places which might have been served by a railway.

Later the old posting town of Stamford in Lincolnshire, for example, resisted the possibility of having a station on what is now the East Coast Main Line from London to Edinburgh and Inverness, with the result

The terminus at Stockton, the world's first railway station, opened in 1825.

The site of St John's Well at Stockton. The first rail, we are told, was 'laid where the figure stands'.

that nearby Peterborough became the bustling interchange that it is today. On the other hand, those who seek the quieter life and a return to the 'old ways' may well have been done an unwitting service by the councillors of Stamford a century and a half ago.

When the Stockton & Darlington – or Quakers' Line – had passed Parliament, George Stephenson became its engineer and provided the locomotive engines. The line was opened on Tuesday 27 September 1825. Pease himself said that the scene at the opening baffled description; many who were to take part in the event could not sleep during the previous night and rose at midnight. People cheered or looked nervous, according to temperament. The procession moved off, the train moved on, preceded by a man on a horse, reaching a speed of eight miles an hour. Number One was driven by Stephenson himself. It pulled six loaded wagons, a passenger 'coach', 21 coal wagons crammed with passengers, and six more filled with coal – a considerable load.

The excitement was intense. On went the pilot, after him the train. All along the road and embankment were crowds – rushing, running, riding, cheering, galloping along, in sight of the train till Stephenson, telling the horse pilot to get out of the road, put on steam and soon left the excited multitudes panting in the rear.

The first train on the Stockton & Darlington Railway, 1825.

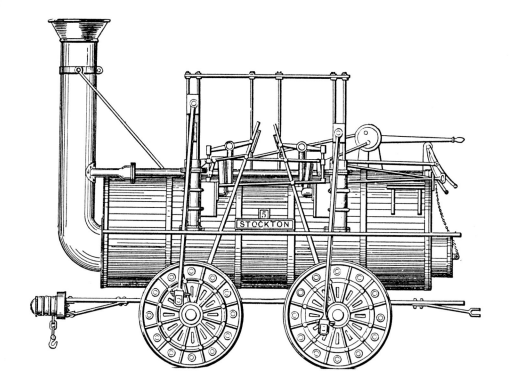

Stockton No 5, built in 1826, had a vertical cylinder driving each of its four wheels.

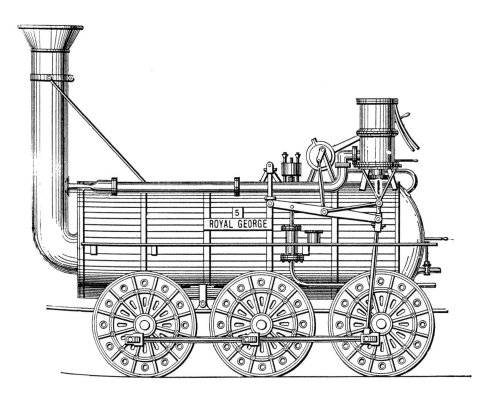

Timothy Hackworth, 'that skilful and conscientious mechanic', rebuilt *Stockton No 5* as *Royal George* in 1827. He mounted it on six coupled wheels driven by two cylinders. He made a number of other improvements, and the locomotive was run on the Stockton & Darlington line until 1840, when it was sold for more than it had originally cost.

Experiment (1825), the first railway passenger coach pressed into service when the unsuspected demand was revealed.

Perseus after exploding. Generally, locomotives didn't explode unless someone tampered with the safety valve. According to a contemporary writer: 'The explosion of a locomotive is, considering the number of engines in constant use, a very rare occurrence, and is probably in all cases owing to the sudden generation of a large quantity of steam, and not to an excessive pressure produced gradually... When an explosion does take place, the enormous force of the agent we are dealing with when we bottle up steam in an iron vessel is shown by the effects produced.' On one occasion, a fireman could stand the hiss of escaping steam no longer, and tied the safety valve shut – with disastrous results.

Although it was used at first only for merchandise and coal traffic, the Stockton & Darlington line was a tremendous success. It soon became the norm for passengers to be carried, and in time the railway created the town of Middlesbrough on Tees.

The Manchester & Liverpool line

Notwithstanding the obvious success of the Stockton–Darlington line, the company running the Liverpool–Manchester canal made no attempt to improve their service. The Liverpool & Manchester Railway was therefore projected, marking the true beginning of railroad enterprise in Britain. As became usual, a prospectus was issued in proper form and a Parliamentary Committee sat on it for a considerable time.

The Committee was considering the Bill while the Stockton & Darlington line was being built. The chairman concluded that a speed of three-and-a-half to four-and-a-half mph (5.6–7.2 kph) would be safe; George Stephenson declared that 12mph (19.2 kph) could safely be attained. If that were not enough, he also proposed to take the line across Chat Moss, a spongy peat bog, a course described as 'the scheme of a madman; ignorance almost inconceivable'. Stephenson succeeded by floating the railway on huge quantities of brushwood and ballast. He afterwards said that he had never had a moment's doubt about the success of his bold schemes, but it is difficult to believe that he slept soundly every night as more and more effort was poured into what everyone else saw as an intractable problem

Even on the established Stockton & Darlington line the greater part of the haulage was done by horses, and it needed all George Stephenson's powers to persuade the directors to adopt the locomotive on the Liverpool & Manchester railway. Opposition to the railway was now transferred to the locomotives; all sorts of stories were put about to try to turn public opinion against them – sparks from the engines would devastate the countryside, fumes would destroy the vegetation, birds would be killed, children terrified, cattle and horses frightened, thousands of people killed by boilers bursting – all in all, the railway and all that went with it was totally dangerous. The Duke of Cleveland objected because it was intended to run the line through a fox cover; Eton College objected because the smoke would blacken all the country round and encourage the boys to play truant. The *Quarterly Review* had deemed all these schemes visionary and unworthy of notice.

The gross exaggerations of the powers of the locomotive, in plain English, the steam carriage, may delude for a time, but must end in the mortification of those concerned. We should as soon expect the people to suffer themselves to be fired off on one of Congreve's ricochet rockets as trust themselves to the mercy of such a machine going at such a rate – viz 12 miles [18 km] an hour!

Thus were terrible evils, deaths, and danger predicted, but after a visit to Newcastle the directors concluded that horses would be of no use to their line and suggested a compromise – stationary engines.

Meanwhile suggestions flowed in: to reduce the friction so low that the train could be drawn by means of a silk thread; to apply power sufficient to 'rend cables asunder'; to use steam, gas, columns of water, and of mercury, with compressed air, and the application of the air pump to create a vacuum; 'machines working in a circle, without fire or steam generating power, at one end of the process, and giving it out at the other'; carriages which conveyed their own railway; 'wheels within wheels to multiply power' and many others. Notwithstanding all this, the majority of the Liverpool & Manchester directors decided to run locomotives and the famous Rainhill Trials were set up with a prize of £500 to select the most suitable.

The Trials took place on 6 October 1829. The level piece of railroad extended for nearly two miles (3.2

Bramley & Parker's British patent no 6,027 of 1830 is similar in principle to Brandreth's *Cyclopede*, the horse-powered locomotive disqualified at the Rainhill Trials. Gearing enables the horse to travel in the direction in which it is facing. There are obvious problems such as the danger of the horse stumbling, or wanting to take a rest.

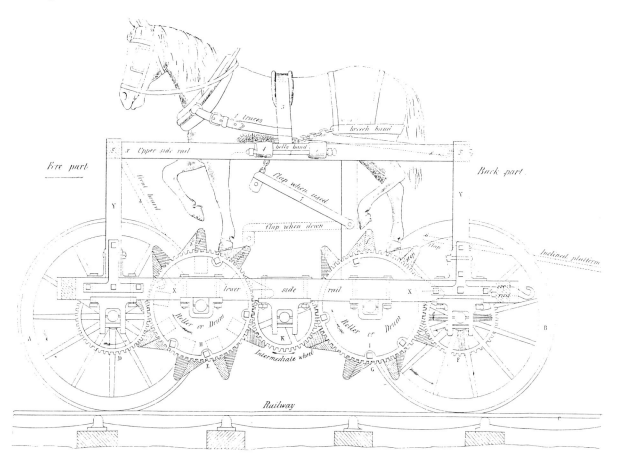

Rocket had a single driving wheel on each side, coupled to a steam cylinder on either side of the firebox. The locomotive was modified after the Rainhill Trials, and the cylinders as shown are now at much less of an angle to the horizontal.

Inset
The appearance of *Rocket* at the Rainhill Trials, showing the earlier position of the cylinders.

km) – one and a half miles (2.4 km) for the speed run, and one eighth of a mile at each end for starting and stopping. Five engines were advertised as competing, but Mr Birstall's *Perseverance* broke down on the way, and Mr Brandreth's *Cyclopede* was disqualified because it was powered by a horse. The trial was between between Stephenson's *Rocket*, Hackworth's *Sans Pareil* and Braithwaite & Ericsson's *Novelty*. The *Rocket* bore off the prize, and the triumph of the locomotive engine was assured.

'The scene of the experiments was extraordinary.

Every inch of space was occupied by every sort of person from every town and city. Some came to scoff, others to applaud, but all were of the same mind afterwards, agreeing that the fiery horse was a new force in history and commerce.' The trials continued for several days until the final test and the triumph of *Rocket* which attained a speed of just over 29 mph (46 kph). The engine driver, Charles Fox, came to notice again in 1851 as builder of the Crystal Palace for the Great Exhibition.

The successful opening of the Manchester &

Another view of Stephenson's *Rocket*, winner of the Rainhill Trials in 1829. The thin, snaking exhaust pipes taking steam to the chimney in order to create a steam blast are a prominent feature.

Timothy Hackworth's *Sans Pareil* is similar to *Royal George*. Hackworth was a fine engineer who set up his own locomotive works at Shildon in Northumberland. But he was a retiring man, deeply religious, and devoid of the business instinct which was one of the reasons for Stephenson's greatness.

First-class train (above) and second-class train (below) on the Liverpool & Manchester Railway, 1837. The third-class carriages were even more basic. It is an interesting commentary on society of the time that three classes of travel were thought to be necessary.

Top left

Messrs Braithwaite & Ericsson's *Novelty*, which travelled at over 24 mph (39 kph) at the Rainhill Trials – until the bellows gave out.

Bottom left

A non-engineering artist's impression of trains passing on the lines crossing Chat Moss. George Stephenson's choice of the route across the bog was regarded as 'ignorance almost inconceivable' – until he succeeded.

Stephenson's *Experiment*, another model with external inclined cylinders, this time with coupled wheels.

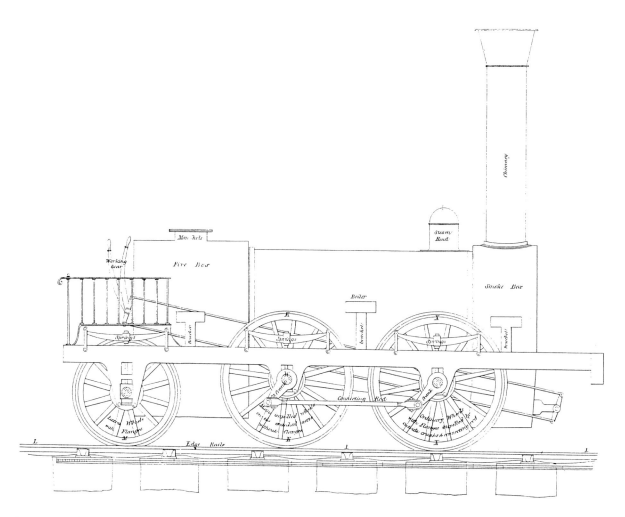

George Stephenson's British patent for a steam locomotive, no 6,484 of 1830. The design provides for cylinders mounted inside the chassis frame, and escapes from the early 'primitive' look. However, what are described as the 'main impelled wheels on the cranked axle' (the 'middle' wheels) are without flanges.

Liverpool line on 15 September 1830 was succeeded by a plethora of railways – many projected, some built. Opposition to new lines, however, continued to be strong and influential. Surveys had to be made when property owners were away and when parsons were at church. Northampton would not have the proposed line at any price, so the line had to be run through the hill in which the celebrated Kilsby Tunnel became a monument to the ability of Robert Stephenson. Oxford and Eton distinguished themselves by opposing Brunel and his Great Western Railway. Well-known figures vowed that they would never travel by rail; people made wills leaving relatives money provided that they would not travel by rail; one testator directed that none of the promoters of a certain railway should ever be entertained in his house after his death, nor should their sons have any food or drink there.

The railways spread

Notwithstanding all this, railroads continued to spread, though the results of opposition are all too clear in cities such as London, whose railway termini are separated as it were by the results of a 'big bang'. People still feared the steam locomotive; at first the engines of the Birmingham railway had to stop at Camden Town and were run in to Euston Square with ropes – a plan also adopted in the tunnel where trains entered Lime Street, Liverpool. The London & Southampton Line was completed to Vauxhall; the Great Western stopped at Paddington, the Northern & Midland at King's Cross & St Pancras, the Great Eastern at Liverpool Street, the Kent & Sussex at London Bridge and so on. The North Western and Great Western Railways should have united at Willesden, but Brunel introduced the broad gauge and made Paddington his terminus instead.

The railroads of America started slightly later than those of Britain. The first rail of the Baltimore & Ohio

Section of a locomotive similar to that shown in Stephenson's patent. The firebox, multi-tube boiler and internal cylinders and cranks are all clearly seen.

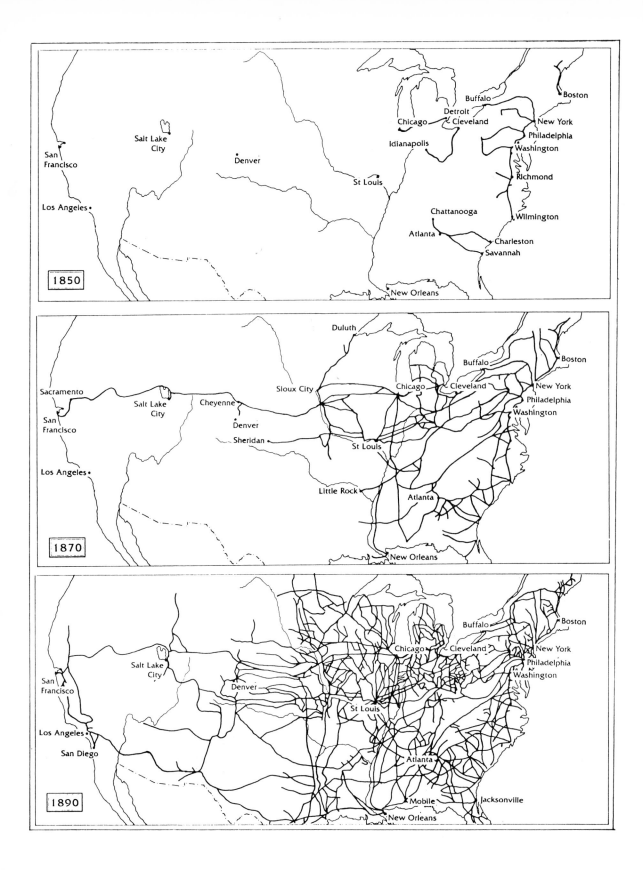

Opposite
The growing American railroad network: 1850, 1870 and 1890.

Growth of the railways in the United States to 1900		
Date	Miles	km
1830	23	37
1840	2,818	4,535
1850	9,021	14,518
1860	30,635	49,302
1870	52,914	85,157
1880	93,296	150,145
1890	163,597	263,284
1900	193,346	311,160

line was laid on 4 July 1828 by Charles Carrold, the only man then living who had signed the Declaration of Independence in 1776. Seventeen miles (27.4 km) of the Mohawk & Hudson (Albany–Schenectady) were opened in 1831, and by 1835 three lines had been built out of Boston – to Providence, Lowell and Worcester; by 1841, the last was extended to Albany.

Railroad building in the south began in South Carolina, with a line 137 miles (220 km) in length connecting Charleston and Hamburg. When it was opened in 1834 it was (for a short time) the world's longest railroad.

The Civil War slowed most railroad building, except for the Union–Central Pacific line, built between 1864 and 1869 and supported by money and grants of land from the US government because of its military importance. The lines met at Promontory, Utah, and the occasion was marked by driving in the legendary 'Golden Spike' on 10 May 1869 – to be whisked away again for safe keeping.

Peter Cooper's experimental locomotive *Tom Thumb* (1830) drawing one of the earliest types of American passenger car. The tubes in the locomotive boiler were made from gun barrels. The 1.5 hp *Tom Thumb* travelled at 18 mph (29 kph).

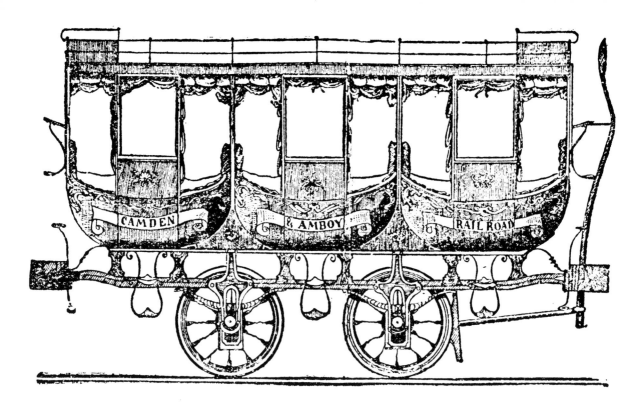

Carriage for the Camden & Amboy Railroad built by M P and M E Green, of Hoboken, NJ, 1831. Springs are fitted, and there is a safety brake.

In America, as in Britain, early coaches were adapted from road vehicles. These cars appeared at the formal opening of the Mohawk & Hudson Railroad – the first link of the New York Central System – on 5 July 1831.

The first locomotive built for service in America, the *Best Friend,* hauling the first excursion train on the South Carolina Railroad, 15 January 1831. The 4hp *Best Friend* weighed four tons. It pulled 50 passengers in six cars at 21 mph (34kph). It is not clear whether the military presence is for protection or pageantry.

De Witt Clinton (1831) from the West Point Foundry, the first locomotive on the Mohawk & Hudson Railroad.

William T James's
experimental locomotive
for the Baltimore & Ohio
Railroad, 1831.

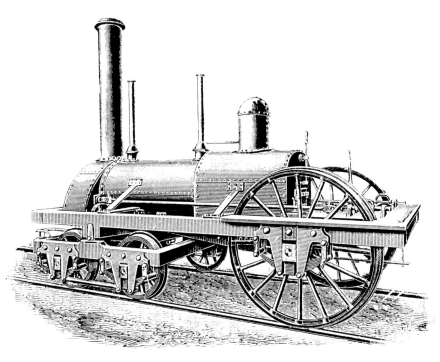

The *Experiment* (1832),
built by John B Jervis for
the Mohawk & Hudson
Railroad, was the first to
have a front 'truck' or
'bogie'. *Experiment* later
became *Brother Jonathan*
and was rebuilt with
eight wheels.

NEWCASTLE AND FRENCHTOWN
RAIL-ROAD.

Well-loaded Imlay coaches on the Newcastle & Frenchtown Railroad, 1833.

The *General* (1855), one of America's best-known locomotives, and a hero of the Civil War, built by Rogers for the Western & Atlantic Railroad.

Some effects of the railways

It was not foreseen that vast numbers of people who had scarcely travelled before would begin to use the railway as passengers. Within a few years, the railroads of Britain began to drive the coaches off the road and the mail contractors were in a quandary. The government was nervous; coach passengers were now travelling by railway and the cost of the mail contract had to be increased substantially to make a profit. In 1838, a Parliamentary Select Committee met to consider the matter and, although the companies denied the right of the Crown to send mail by private enterprise, it was declared that the railways 'bound the land in bonds of iron' and the Committee decided to transfer mail transport to the railways.

The social effects of the railway were far reaching. Coach services died and the industries immediately

Opening up the West: the difficulties confronting the railroad engineer in the canyons of the Sierra Nevada – such as Death Valley, Black Hole and Last Chance. The line of the old Denver & Rio Grande Railroad seen here was finished in 1889.

The illustrations to Forsyth's British patent no 10,905 of 1845, 'Improvements in signals &c', throw an interesting light on the instantly-recognizable railway architecture of the period. Unlike those in many other countries, British trains were boarded from platforms, which helped to keep passengers off the tracks.

Forsyth's improvements were ingenious in theory, but less so in practice. The signal gantry shown on the left in the main picture carries an array of lamps which may be displayed or suppressed by means of shutters operated by vertical rods. The locomotives carry distinctive arrays of lamps as shown in the pictures. The driver knows what lamps his engine is carrying, and then knows, from the lamps displayed on the gantry, which signals apply to him. Judging from his representations of the engines, Forsyth was not much of an engineer.

connected with them suffered. Inns closed, and everyone concerned with horses – right through to manufacturers of stable brooms and brushes – felt the change. Clergymen complained they could not persuade their parishioners to come to church – because they preferred to watch the trains. Such phrases as 'getting up steam' and 'running off the rails' entered the language. People travelled about more freely, produce was conveyed more rapidly, and the supply of milk increased to such an extent that it became a hindrance to traffic and a nuisance to passengers.

Queen Victoria first travelled by railway in 1842. On Waterloo Day (18 June) that year, the Queen took her first trip on the Great Western Railway – from Slough to Paddington – though Prince Albert had already used the line several times. Her Majesty's subsequent journeys were long and frequent. Even the great Duke of Wellington, the 'Iron Duke' who avoided railways after the opening of the Liverpool–Manchester line, recognized the 'iron horse' in 1843. Such events all helped finally to break down the weakening opposition to railway travel.

In America, the railroads were generally welcomed, as they helped to open up the 'Great American Desert' between the Rocky Mountains and the Mississippi–Missouri Rivers. As the network spread, it helped immigrants to settle and develop the country. Small settlements grew into large towns. Precious and semiprecious metals could be taken east in safety, and cattle and wheat could be taken to market. In the other direction, the railroads supplied the settlers with their needs – food for body and mind.

A section of railway, showing an embankment, a solidly ornate bridge and telegraph wires. It was a happy chance that the railway, and the telegraph which enabled it to transmit messages which travelled faster than the trains, developed more or less hand in hand. Train timetables assume a standard time, and the telegraph enabled clocks to be synchronized all over the land. Before that, each settlement had its own local time.

The canals and railways were built by navigators, or 'navvies', a rough breed of men 'whose manners and customs were usually different from those of their hosts'. They lived together 'herding like beasts of the field, owning to no moral law, and feeling no social tie ... They lived only for the present, they cared not for the past, they were indifferent to the future. They were heathens in the midst of a Christian people; savages in the midst of civilization.'

In the first picture navvies are camping in a waiting room – and looking relatively benign. In the second, they are receiving their rations of oatmeal and water – very nourishing no doubt, but perhaps a cause of their legendary hard drinking!

Robert Stephenson (1803–1859), famous son of a famous father, and engineer of the London & Birmingham Railway.

The railway mania

Comparatively few lines were initiated until 1836, when the railway asserted itself and a mania for railway investment and speculation arose. No fewer than five lines were suggested from London to Brighton and the shares of existing railways bounded madly. Even in Parliament, whose members were generally not in favour of railroads, attention was directed to the growing craze.

In the early 1840s, encouraged by the dividends paid by the leading railway companies, people thought

they were as safe an investment as government securities. In 1842 money was easy and fetching but a low rate; the most prudent people therefore looked round for new openings. In 1843–44, some 50 new schemes were put forward and the government had to bring in a bill for their proper regulation as so-called joint stock companies.

The public and the press at last recognized the value of the railways and went to the other extreme. The locomotive engine, far from being a devastating and devouring monster, was now a generous and good-natured giant which would hurt no one. The dangers of the railway were forgotten and it became the safest, best, speediest, and most physically and financially secure invention in the world. Railways were the 'triumphs of a period of peace'; the 'emblems of internal confidence and prosperity'. They were the universal panacea for all ills; employers of labour, great levellers, the true means by which all sorts and conditions could be brought in touch with one another. 'The artisan need no longer remain buried in the country, the agriculturist may find employment in distant places, by railways the whole country may be, and will be, under the blessing of divine providence, cultivated as a garden' – not bad for those who had not so very long before denounced the railroad as the spoiler of the land, the scorcher, the fiery monster which would devastate the kingdom and demoralise the inhabitants.

Stirring times; hardly any scheme was too wild for acceptance. Wherever a line was projected shares went up. Barren and blasted heaths, inaccessible mountains, impassable estuaries and places totally devoid of inhabitants – all had a line. It seems almost incredible that, in spite of public warnings, sensible businessmen should have run such risks. There seemed to be no way of stopping the rush. Money was widely sought after and no investor was satisfied with less than 10 per cent. Business was neglected and everyone rushed in to the market. George Hudson, the 'railway king', warned investors that shares could go down as well as up but

London & Birmingham Railway, Camden Town, April 1837 – building the houses for the stationary engines which would pull the trains into the Euston terminus. The idea was to keep the noise and smoke of the locomotives out of the heart of London.

Four views of the construction of the London & Birmingham Railway

The entrance portico of Euston Grove Station – a fitting gateway to an important railway. Who could fail to be impressed by the grandeur of the enterprise?

Pumps for draining the Kilsby Tunnel. Building it was a near-impossible engineering task because of flooding. The long pump rod from the engine-house is impressive, as is the use of horses walking round and round (top right) to provide motive power.

Building the Watford Embankment, November 1837.

Constructing the Tring Cutting, June 1837. Before mechanization, earth was moved by armies of navvies with wheelbarrows.

The English and French
'steam navvies'. The
English machine (above)
scoops from a vertical
face using its bucket.
The French machine
(below) has a chain of
buckets which scrape
material up and transfer
it to the wagons of the
waiting train.

nobody listened to him.

The railway mania desolated many an English home. In America, too, there were five years of feverish speculation when railroad expansion resumed after the Civil War in 1868. In those five years, the railway mileage increased by 40 per cent before panic set in in 1873. Only 11,500 miles were added in the next five years.

The madness spread throughout England as companies genuine and speculative rushed to deposit their plans. Hundreds of penniless people speculated thousands, rendering themselves liable for payment which they had neither the means nor the intention of making. Some of them made large sums by selling their shares before they had paid for them, but when the Bank of England raised the interest rate, money be-

Left

Financier George Hudson, the 'railway king'.

Below

Interior of Wagner sleeping car on the New York Central Line, 1859.

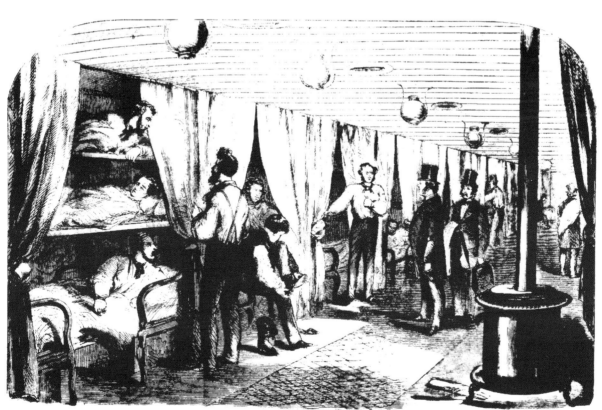

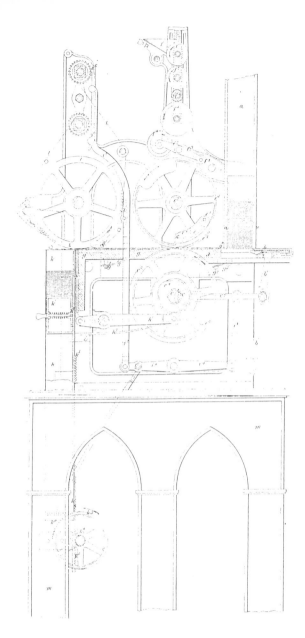

A view of Thomas Edmondson's machine for printing railway tickets, from British patent no 13,007 of 1850. Edmondson's principles were used for well over a century, until the development of computing power made all things possible.

came tighter and the market began to collapse. Panic set in; shares which had been worth £100 yesterday became waste paper. Some thought it prudent to disappear, many committed suicide, children were ruined and parents imprisoned or starved.

Railway tickets

In the days of the stagecoaches, the booking clerk at the coach office gave the guard of the vehicle a paper with particulars of passengers and their journeys, a practice which was adopted by the railways. In 1836, Thomas Edmondson was appointed Station Master at Milton in Cumberland. Using printer's type in a wooden holder, he started to print rows of tickets on strips of cardboard. He cut up the tickets with scissors and stacked them in a box, having numbered them from nought upwards so that the number of the next ticket showed how many had been sold. Edmondson then hit on the idea of a stamp dating the tickets when he issued them; once again he used printer's type and an arrangement with folding jaws so that when the end of the ticket was inserted the date would be printed on it. He suggested to his proprietors, the Newcastle & Carlisle Railway, that they should adopt his system but they wanted nothing to do with it. He therefore approached the Manchester & Leeds Railway who offered to double his salary if he would join them to introduce his system. It was an immediate success, and the demand was so great that, with his brother and a friend, Edmondson set up what was to become a highly successful company for manufacturing railway ticket printing and dating machines.

Stephenson's vision

George Stephenson believed that one of the greatest advantages of railways was that they would bring iron and coal, the staple products of the country, to the doors of all England. 'The strength of Britain' he would say 'lies in her iron and coal beds, and the locomotive is destined, above all other agencies, to bring it forth.'

Stephenson saw:

a stream of steam running directly through the country, from the north to London. Speed is not so much an object as utility and cheapness. It will not do to mix up the heavy merchandise and coal trains with the passenger trains. Coal and most kinds of goods can wait; but passengers will not. A less perfect road and less expensive works will do well enough for

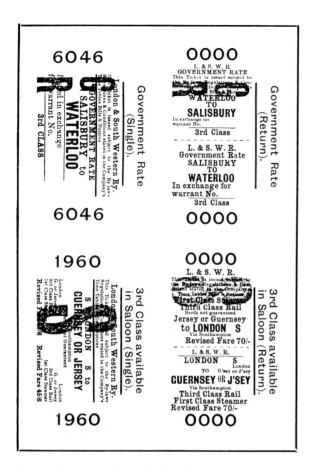

A selection of specimen tickets from the London & South Western Railway Station Masters' Handbook.

coal trains, if run at a low speed; and if the line be flat, it is not of much consequence whether it be direct or not. Whenever you put passenger trains on a line, all the other trains must be run at high speed to keep out of their way. But coal trains run at high speeds pull the road to pieces, besides causing large expenditure in locomotive power; and I doubt very much whether they will pay after all; but a succession of long coal trains, if run at from 10 to 14 mph (16–22 kph), would pay very well. Thus the Stockton & Darlington Company made a larger profit when running coal at low speeds at a ha'penny a ton per mile, than they had been able to do since they put on their fast passenger trains, when everything needs to be run faster, and a much larger proportion of the gross receipts is absorbed by working expenses.'

Because of the conflict between load and speed, Stephenson suggested that there should be railways devoted exclusively to carrying goods and minerals at low speeds – keeping maintenance costs down was the only way that such traffic could be carried at a profit.

Stephenson suggested also that signalling should be 'self-acting' – worked by the locomotives themselves as they passed along the railway. He thought this was so important that it should be enforced by law, even though it was in the interest of the railway companies to adopt such a plan since it would save wear and tear and diminish the risk of railway accidents.

When George Stephenson first predicted that a locomotive could travel at 12 mph (19 kph) people had thought him mad. Later people thought that trains might travel at more than 100 mph (160 kph), and Stephenson was thought behind the times when he recommended the speed to be limited to 40 mph (64 kph). 'I do not like either 40 or 50 mph [64 or 80 kph] upon any line – I think it is an unnecessary speed' he said, 'and if there is danger upon a railway, it is high velocity that creates it. I should say no railway ought to exceed 40 mph [64 kph] on the most favourable gradient; but upon a curved line the speed ought not to exceed 24 or 25 mph [38.4 or 40 kph].' Stephenson had built a GWR locomotive capable of running at 50 mph (80 kph) on load and at 80 mph (128 kph) unloaded, but was convinced that this increased both danger and expense unnecessarily.

Undulating lines

Stephenson was always opposed to unsound theories which would bring discredit on the locomotive system – such as 'undulating lines'. Some said that it was as easy to work a line which went up and down hill as one which was perfectly level; others that the undulating railway was superior to the level one. Stephenson's practice was to build his roads as nearly as possible on the level so that long trains of mineral and merchandise, as well as passengers, might be hauled along them at the least possible expenditure of locomotive power. He had found by experiment that an engine used half its power to ascend a gradient of 1 in 260 and three quarters of its power to ascend one of 1 in 100. As locomotive design improved, and power increased, it was negated by the steeper gradients which the new school of engineers set it to overcome.

Stephenson was always driven by commercial considerations. He had no desire to build up his reputation at the expense of railway shareholders. If railways were to succeed they must be laid out not only to serve their users but also to be worked profitably. They were

Signal post at a junction, dwarfing the train rounding a fancifully tight curve.

Junction signals, tended by a man on duty in a cosy cabin, in touch with his colleagues by telegraph.

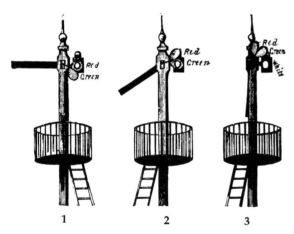

1   2   3

Positions of signals in working; 1 danger, 2 proceed, 3 back view. A clear lamp shines through a red or green filter according to the position of the signal arm. The system is not 'fail-safe' in that a signal arm does not fall to the danger position if something goes wrong.

not – in those days – government roads, but private ventures. Stephenson repeatedly declared that he would have nothing to do with them if he did not think that they could be made to pay. If British railways revert to private enterprise, it will be interesting to see how the philosophies and practices of the new owners compare with those of the original projectors.

The atmospheric railway

The French philosopher Denis Papin (1647–1712) suggested the atmospheric railway – one whose motive power is air pressure – at the end of the 16th century. The idea was not taken up until 1810 when a Mr Medhurst published a pamphlet to prove the practicability of 'carrying letters and goods by air'. In 1824, Mr Valance of Brighton took out a patent for projecting passengers through a tube large enough to contain a train of carriages; the tube being previously exhausted of its atmospheric air (presumably in front of the train only). In 1835, Mr Pinkus (an ingenious American), Dr Dionysius Lardner (an advocate of the undulating railway) and Mr Samuel Clegg (1781–1861 – pioneer of

coal gas) formed an association to build an atmospheric railway. They raised £18,000 and exhibited a model in London.

In one form of atmospheric railway, a pipe is laid between the rails and a piston running in it is attached to the railway vehicle. Air is exhausted from the pipe on the front side of the piston, and the pressure of the atmosphere on the other side of the piston pushes it along. George Stephenson examined the model carefully and observed emphatically: 'It won't do: it is only the fixed engines and ropes over again, in another form; and, to tell you the truth, I don't think this rope of wind will answer so well as the rope of wire did.' Stephenson stood by the locomotive engine and subsequent experience proved him right. In 1840, Clegg and his co-inventor Samuda patented their atmospheric railway and tested it on an unfinished part of the West London Railway.

The results of the experiment were so satisfactory that it was adopted between Dolquay and Kingstown on the Dublin & Kingstown line in Ireland. The London & Croydon Company also adopted the atmos-

A drawing of an aerial pontoon suspension bridge for crossing the English Channel as exhibited by the inventor, Thomas Watts, at the Great Exhibition 1851. The structure is to be supported on hydrogen bags, and is securely tethered to prevent it from taking off, complete with trainloads of passengers.

A propaganda picture supporting the campaign to make the Westinghouse air brake compulsory on American railways. The protagonist was one Lorenzo Coffin, who bombarded the railway companies and politicians with statistics of avoidable accidents for 20 years until, in 1893, the American Congress passed a bill (drafted by Coffin) making continuous air brakes compulsory on all trains in the United States.

pheric principle, opening their line in 1845. Brunel built an atmospheric railway in Devon, but it failed because the greased leather sealing strips on the tube were eaten by rats. Nevertheless, the atmospheric system was highly popular but still George Stephenson said: 'It won't do: it's but a gimcrack.' Engineers of distinction said he was prejudiced and that he looked upon the locomotive as his own pet child. 'Wait a little' replied Stephenson 'and you will see that I am right.' He called the system 'a great humbug', and never believed that it would pay. It was ingenious, clever, scientific, and all that; but railways were commercial enterprises, not toys; and if the atmospheric railway would not work to a profit, it would not do.

The atmospheric railway had more than a fair trial and it was found wanting. In 1844, Robert Stephenson (1803–59) went to look at the Kingstown Atmospheric Railway to see whether the motive power might be applicable for working the Chester & Holyhead Rail-

way, then under construction; in his 'Report on the Atmospheric Railway System' he came out against it.

Tailpiece

At an age when he might have retired, George Stephenson continued to make improvements to locomotives and brakes. In 1841, examined before the Select Committee on Railways, he said that he thought the self-acting brake was the most important arrangement for increasing the safety of railway travel. His idea was to use the momentum of the running train to apply the brakes if the moving power of the engine were checked. Such brakes would also be controlled by the guard by means of a connecting line running along the whole length of the train. In due time the 'rope of wind' came into its own as the operating force of the air brakes used today.

George Stephenson died in 1848. His reputation fed on itself for, in the days when the opposition to rail-

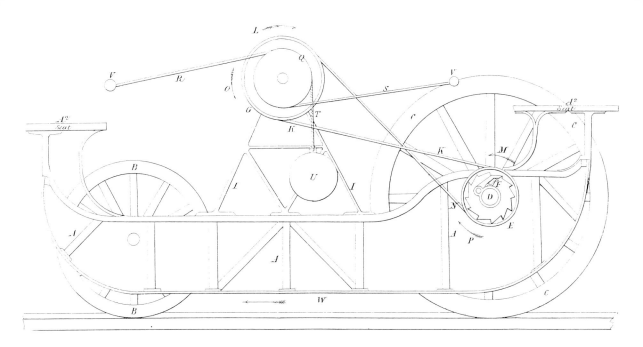

Pim and Bergin's apparatus (British patent no 7,352 of 1837) uses the muscle power of people seated on the seats and pulling on the ropes with handles at VV to propel it via the crossed belt K and the ratchet mechanism in the hub of the right hand wheel. The weight U rewinds the propulsion ropes RS, but some of the energy of the propellers would be dissipated in raising it.

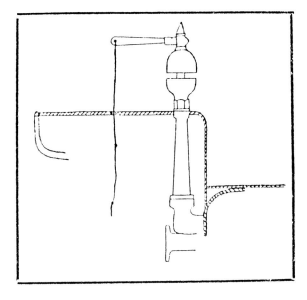

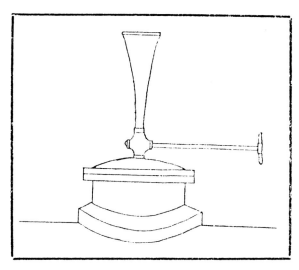

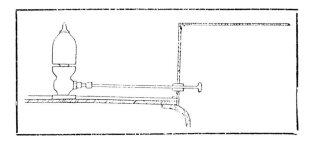

A selection of steam trumpets and whistles, used for warning people of the approach of the locomotive.

ways was at its fiercest, it was necessary for parliamentary and advertising purposes to represent him as an authority on every branch of engineering. He was not the 'father of the railway engine' – that honour is Richard Trevithick's – nor was he 'the inventor of the railways' – they were there long before he was born. But he may justly be thought of as 'the father of the railways', for his knowledge of the whole matter, derived from the machines and the men who made them, was immense and his organizing powers remarkable. He was at the front all through the fight to establish railways, the one conspicuous figure to whom the railway men looked for leadership. The storm centred on him and it is to him more than any other man that the foundations of today's railways are due.

A bank holiday sketch (Punch – 1901): 'Change 'ere, 'ave we? Then kindly oblige me with a sardine-opener.' Travelling to the sea-side was a popular outing, enhanced by the provision of 'Parliamentary trains', which had to run daily at a cut-price fare so that everyone could afford to travel, though not necessarily in first-class comfort.